IN-A-GADDA-DA-ENGLAND
EDWARD THOMPSON

Foreword
Diane Smyth

"In-A-Gadda-Da-Vida" is a psychedelic song by the American band Iron Butterfly, released in 1968; the lyrics were meant to refer to the Garden of Eden but, the story goes, the lead singer was so drunk the first time he played it, his slurred words sounded like Vida [or "life"]. Edward Thompson has adapted the title for this book but replaced Vida with England, the place where he grew up and lives. More specifically he lives in Kent, a south-eastern county known as the "Garden of England" and where he shot many of the images.

In-A-Gadda-Da-England is a subjective body of work made over the last 20 years, from when Thompson was a young man to now, when he's reaching middle age and married with two children. The book includes an image of Thompson's father shortly before he died, and a photograph of the place his ashes were scattered. It includes an image of Thompson's neighbours standing in their garden. But it also includes shots taken in London, Birmingham, Devon, and Luton, and photographs of politicians and protests. It's a portrait of England, not Kent, but it's relevant it's rooted in Kent. The last 20 years have been tumultuous for the UK, with the growth of a nationalism that led the country to leave Europe on the 31st January 2020. This nationalism is a defining feature of our time, and Kent has been one of its hothouses. The county closest to Europe, Kent is where migrants land when they're crossing the channel, and its coastal towns have seen many far-right protests. People in Kent overwhelmingly voted to leave the EU; in Thanet, northeast Kent, 63.8% of the electorate voted pro-Brexit, in fact, at a time when the UK Independence Party was the district council's largest party. Thompson doesn't directly show this. Instead he documents everyday life. There are photographs of kids, cats and beauty queens, WW2 battle re-enactments, and St George's Day parades. Images taken elsewhere pick up similar themes, a photograph of a far-right protestor in London honing in on his tattoo of St George and the Dragon for example.

Thompson freely mixes the chronology of his images through the book, but they feature a curiously vertiginous jumble of time anyway. It's most obvious with the battle re-enactors, but it's also there in the streets, in the futuristic skyscrapers behind a traditional wicker man procession in the City of London. There's a shot of far-right protestors in Birmingham climbing on a statue of Matthew Boulton, James Watt, and William Murdoch, figures from the Industrial Revolution that changed Birmingham and Britain so much; the sculpture was designed in 1938, erected in 1956, and newly gilded in 2006.

Thompson took the photograph in 2013. The way the protestors are climbing also projects forward though, evoking the summer of 2020 and a very different demonstration in Bristol, West England, that brought down a statue of a slave-trader.

In fact there's a weird prescience in Thompson's photography, which is also at work in other images. There's a shot of two environmental protestors wearing full hazmat suits which was taken in 2012 but now seems to augur Covid. Thompson believes this foresight is born of the intensity with which he perceives the present, that, if he looks hard enough, he can find decisive moments that connect with larger narratives. He speaks of this sense in terms of magic or a heightened state, and it's one of the reasons he was attracted to Iron Butterfly's song. "In-A-Gadda-Da-Vida" is a track born of the psychedelic era and the idea there's knowledge in altered states.

But perhaps this supernatural insight also evokes something written by William Shakespeare, the English playwright apocryphally born on St George's Day. "If you can look into the seeds of time, and say which grain will grow and which will not," says Banquo in Shakespeare's play Macbeth, begging three witches to tell him the future. What's next is evolving from what's now, Shakespeare suggests, if you only know where to look. *In-A-Gadda-Da-England* is very obviously about a certain place, a journey through a region just as, in the original song, Adam urges Eve to take his hand "and walk this land". But it's also a book about time.

Somewhere in Kent, school kids marched with flags and white horses to mark St George's Day in 2019;

somewhere in Birmingham, English Defence League protestors climbed onto a statue in 2013. Thompson's father sat in the sun in 2007, shortly before he died; in 2018, a particular woman was crowned Miss Faversham. Somehow these events grew from the past, and elements of them will continue to blossom in future. Things not evident now will look like forerunners with time.

And in this way *In-A-Gadda-Da-England* suggests another garden, the garden of forking paths from a short story of the same name by Jorge Luis Borges. The story features a novel that uses the garden as a conceit; each path is a journey through time, each fork symbolises a moment that could go different ways. The novel describes every alternative moment, and the moments that stem from them, and the moments from them, and so on, until it becomes a labyrinth. It's an idea that recurred in the many worlds concept of quantum physics, which suggests there are many universes spinning off from each other, whenever a seed of time grows differently.

Somewhere, maybe, there's an England where the Brexit vote went another way, where the UK voted to stay 52% to 48%. Perhaps there's a world where far-right protestors didn't climb on a statue, or a different beauty queen won Miss Faversham. It could be, somewhere, that Britain didn't win the war. In the here and now, there are these photographs and the seeds of what's coming next. "Then I reflected that all things happen, happen to one, precisely now," says the narrator in Borges' Garden. "Century follows century, and things happen only in the present."

A house where the Christmas decorations never come down (2004)
Hythe, Kent

Millie walks home past the local nuclear powerstation (2011)
Dungeness, Kent

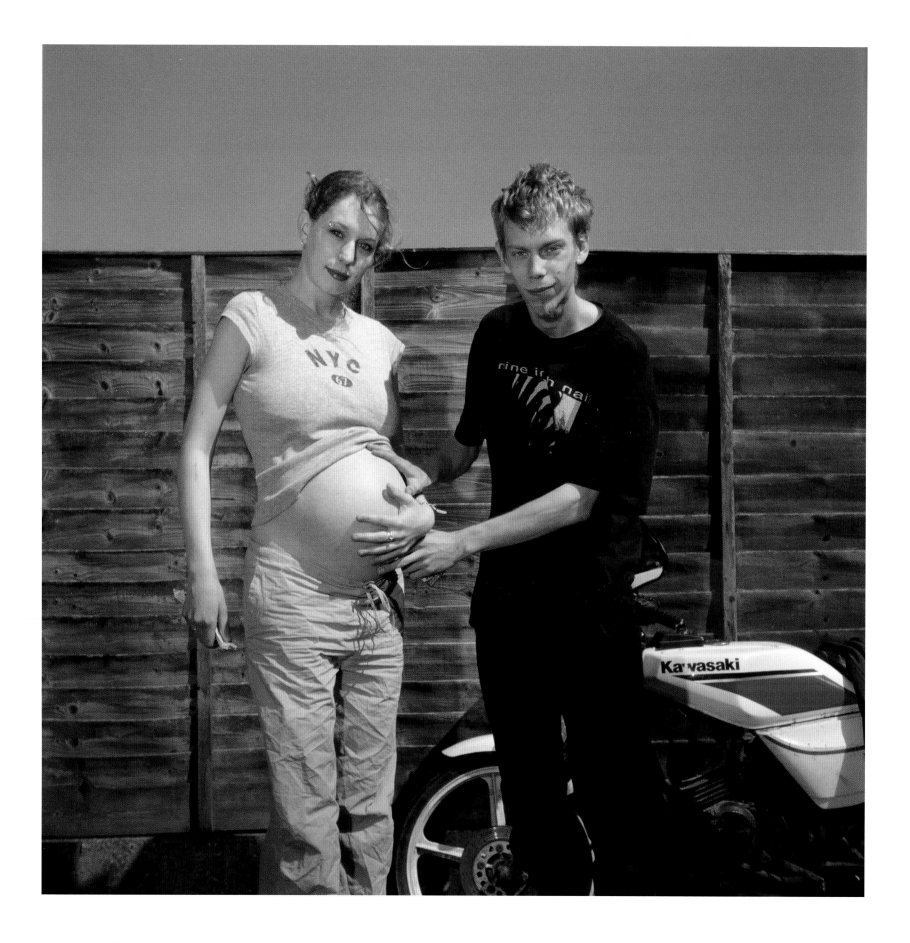

Donna & Stef (2003)
Dymchurch, Kent

Sally & Stewart (2008)
St Leonards on Sea, East Sussex

A boy blinded by the sun (2002)
Maidstone, Kent

Lupinus, of the wolf (2018)
The Isle of Sheppey, Kent

A man shows off his Chameleon to passersby (2018)
Broadstairs, Kent

A man walks into a bear (2017)
Margate, Kent

T-Sign (2010)
Dungeness, Kent

Dave and Rouge (2010)
Dungeness, Kent

St George's Day Parade (2019)
Gravesend, Kent

English Defence League (2011)
Aldgate, London

Cob House (2011)
Totnes, Devon

Topiary Man (2021)
Broadstairs, Kent

Environmental protesters (2012)
Leyton, London

The Garden Gate Project (2017)
Margate, Kent

The Garden Gate Project (2017)
Margate, Kent

Protestors at Extinction Rebellion (2020)
Westminster, London

The Lord Mayor's Show (2017)
The City of London, London

Michael Tierney, Proprietor (2009)
The Windsor Castle Pub, London

The Lord Mayor's Show (2017)
The City of London, London

Clown children (2017)
The City of London, London

The Chap Olympiad (2010)
Bedford Square Gardens, London

The Candlelight Club (2009)
Shoreditch, London

Margate Parade (2017)
Margate, Kent

The English Defence League (2010)
Luton, Bedfordshire

Dog Show at Ellington Park Fair (2017)
Ramsgate, Kent

Intrepid (2018)
Ramsgate, Kent

Islay Trader vs Anthony Gormley: Another Time (2018)
Margate, Kent

Dame Kelly Holmes (2011)
Canterbury, Kent

Captured V2 Rocket (2006)
Paddock Wood, Kent

Living Historians (2006)
Paddock Wood, Kent

Untitled (2017)
Ramsgate, Kent

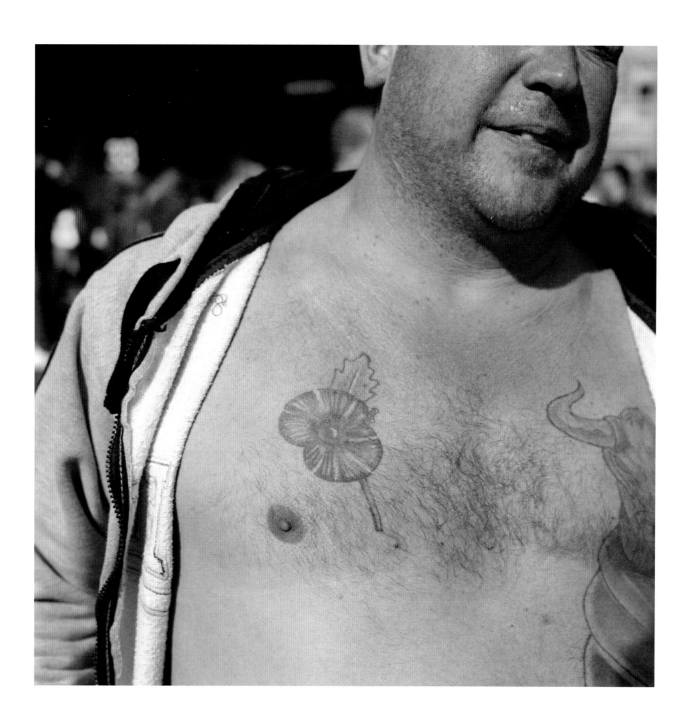

WW2 British Tommies (2009)
Paddock Wood, Kent

Remembrance poppy tattoo (2013)
Aldgate, London

The Olympic Park (2012)
Stratford, London

The Royal Wedding (2011)
Westminster, London

The Golden Boys (2013)
Birmingham, West Midlands

The Brexit Party (2019)
Kensington, London

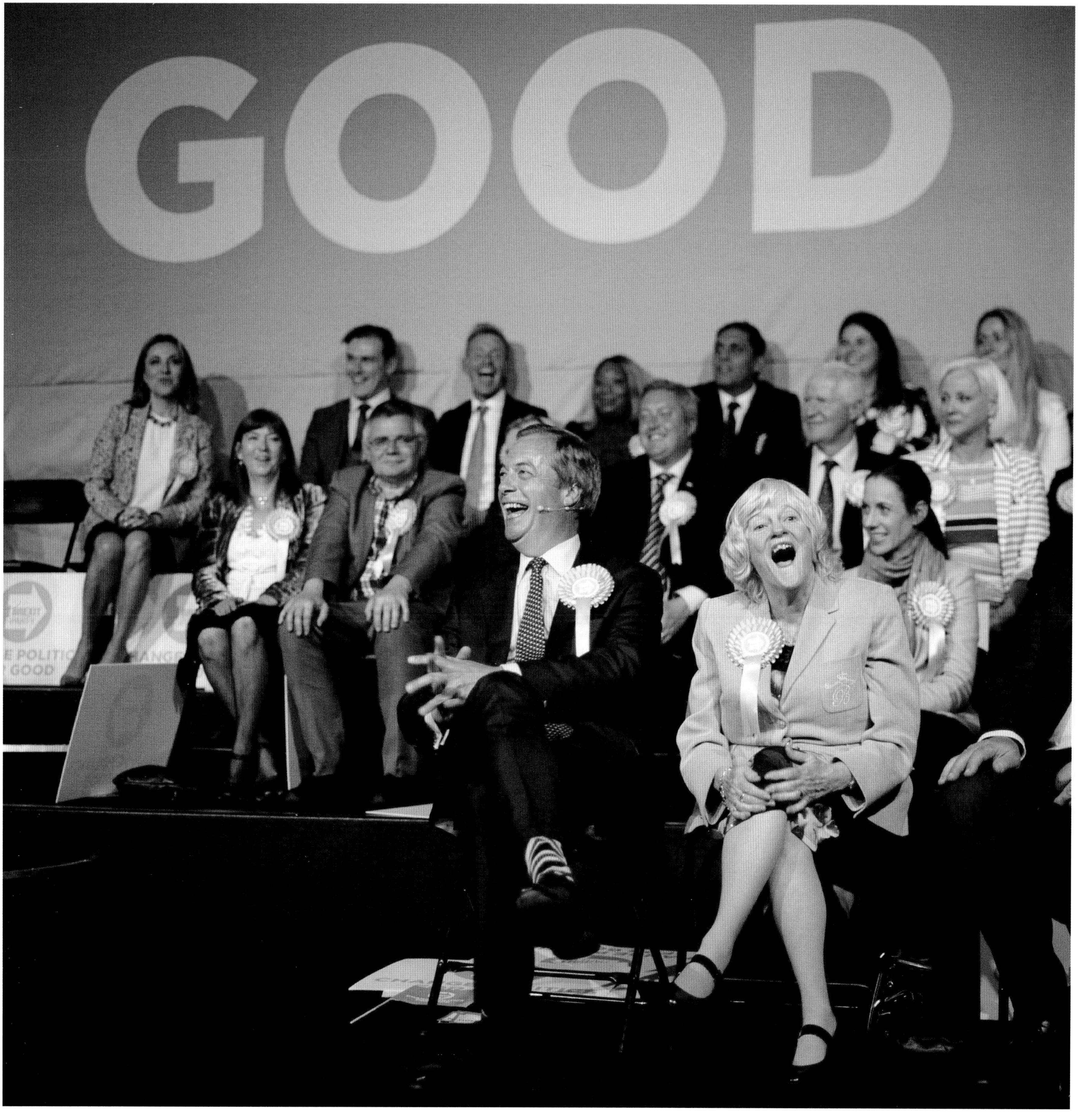
GOOD
E POLITIC
GOOD

A cat that looked like Hitler (2020)
Ramsgate, Kent

Stormtrooper (2019)
Herne Bay, Kent

Outside the Justice Centre (2010)
Nuneaton, Warwickshire

Car crash on Island Road (2009)
Sturry, Kent

Fellow photographer (2019)
Hoxton, London

Untitled (2018)
Margate, Kent

Untitled (2018)
Margate, Kent

St Eanswythe's Churchyard (2004)
Folkestone, Kent

The morning after St Valentine's Day (2004)
Maidstone, Kent

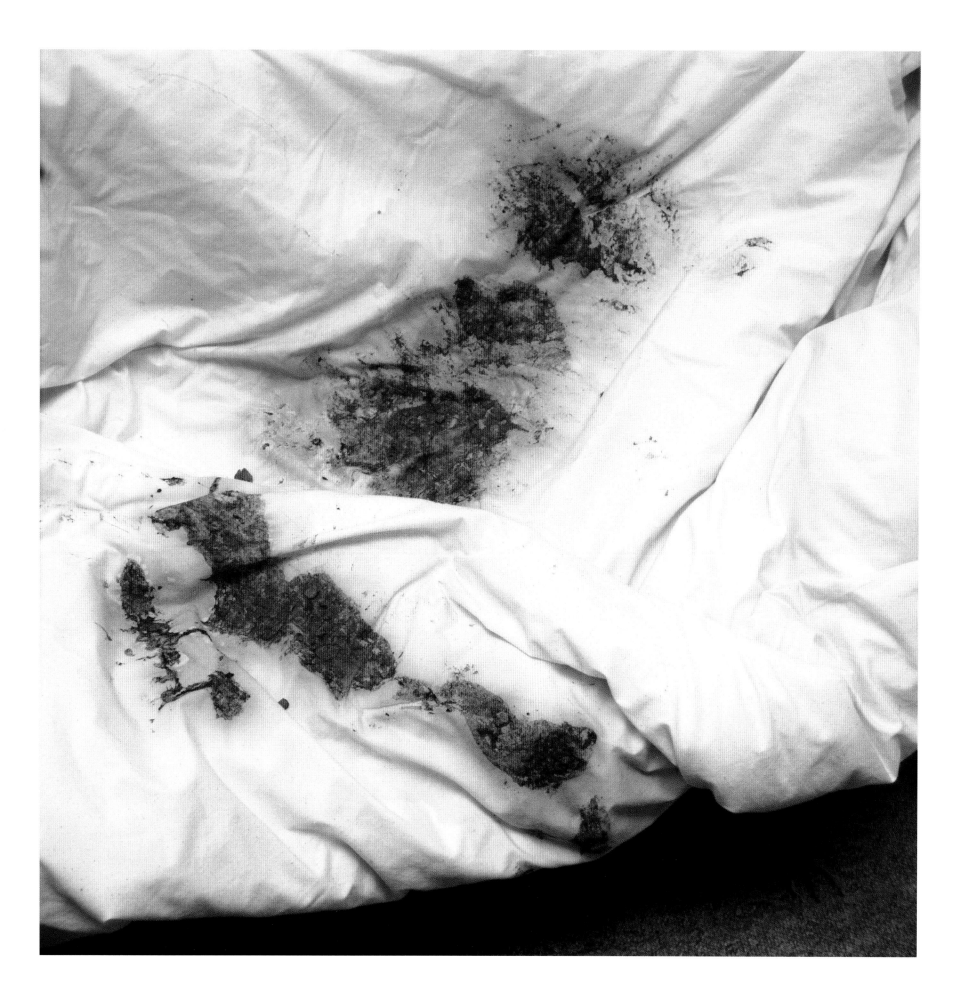

Barbara, the ex-battery farm hen (2010)
Ashford, Kent

Stefan and the free-range hens (2002)
Dymchurch, Kent

Window Tax (2017)
Margate, Kent

Dad clearing out the garage just before he died (2007)
Sandgate, Kent

His doppelganger by Dungeness A+B nuclear power stations (2010)
Dungeness, Kent

A redcoat soldier guards a fiat (2018)
Dymchurch, Kent

Tidal Pool (2018)
Margate, Kent

Carrie hangs out the washing (2011)
Dungneness, Kent

St George's Day Parade (2019)
Gravesend, Kent

Miss Faversham (2018)
Margate, Kent

The Lookout Cafe (2019)
Ramsgate, Kent

Richard Woods, Holiday Home (2017)
Folkestone, Kent

Banksy, Pedal to Paris (2018)
Dover, Kent

Untitled (2019)
Ramsgate, Kent

Pat & Peter, The Friends of Ellington Park (2018)
Ramsgate, Kent

Untitled (2008)
Deal, Kent

Elsie (2006)
Dymchurch, Kent

Wayne (2006)
New Romney, Kent

I love you forever (2009)
Samphire Hoe, Kent

The white cliffs, the port of Dover (2017)
Dover, Kent

In Conversation
David Campany
Edward Thompson

David: Edward, you mention in your introduction your search for "the soul of England", but then switch things a little to a search within yourself. There's something in the tone of your photographs, veering between affectionate and distanced, that reminds me of Bill Brandt's photography of the 1930s, particularly his book *The English at Home*. The English often seem faux-naive, trapped in class rituals, sleepwalking, unaware or uninterested in the wider world beyond and their place within it. Whose England is this?

Edward: In 2002 I was using photography as a way of exploring. Seeing places and witnessing lives I wouldn't normally encounter. That's where the search for a country's soul and the individual soul meet. You don't learn about yourself in isolation. From the beginning I set out to subvert reality. Not through constructed fine art photography, as seemed to be the trend when I was a student, but through the documentation of everyday life as observed by a documentary photographer. Through timing and chance you can make the everyday seem like something more, something mythic. To imbue normality with such focus and significance that it elevates its meaning. The comic book writer Grant Morrison said that 'Life + Significance = Magic'. When I photograph I look with intent, in a way I believe I am imbuing significance into everyday life.

The '*veering between affectionate and distanced,*' comes from my need to go and photograph people versus the awkwardness I experience just before I start

Kensington Children's party (1934) Bill Brandt

photographing. I think there's something very English about that. Before I begin photographing, even the most mundane thing, I feel like I am in fight or flight mode. I've learned over the years to method act through this fear and it has held me in good stead when in the middle of screaming rioters or encountering far right protestors. For me photography is a struggle and yet I've done it for twenty years. I think that paranoia, that inner drama, has helped me to photograph some interesting moments that also contain dualism. Whose England is this? It's ours and it's theirs. It's my conscious and my subconscious.

David: Do you like your soul? Do you like the soul of England?

Edward: Well right now it's a little hard to like the *soul of England* isn't it? There seems to be strong polarised forces at work, nationalistic narratives, division, the channelling of hatred away from those responsible. I think recently with Covid we have seen how ignorance can be weaponised. I have hope for the future, but I think we need to try and conquer our fears, or at the least not let those in power use our fears against us. As for my own soul, well I am an oddity in the world of art and photography as I am a committed agnostic. I think my ability to believe is at the core of my ability to conjure. When you shoot with photographic film it is an act of faith as until you develop the film the photographs exist in a state that is both brilliant and terrible. It's like Schrödinger's film camera.

David: Do you feel there are signs of a non-fearful English nationalism in your photographs?

Edward: As in a way of being proud of our English identity without it becoming something sinister and threatening? Yes, for sure there are. In this photo book there are depictions of family gatherings, beautiful moments in everyday life, public art works and climate change protestors. I try and start and end the book positively (birth, family, growth) with a dive into a nationalistic underworld in the middle. The diptych of a crashed car with an England flag and the photographer looking on opposite is like me at the scene of the crime, looking bewildered and damaged. I spent three years dipping in and out of photographing the English Defence League so whenever I see an English flag it conjures up some emotions in me that most people might not have. I think, like a virus, that's probably tainted how I see my country's flag. I don't know if something totemic, like a flag, can ever be reclaimed. But a country is more than a flag.

David: I'm currently living in the US, a country that is either beginning, or knows it must begin the difficult but necessary reckoning with its own past as a slave state. By comparison, England seems a long way from dealing with the consequences of its colonial past, a past that shapes absolutely everything about contemporary England and Englishness, which is why the concepts are so fraught, so full of occlusions and denials. But it's coming, and at least on a subconscious

level England knows it. Do you expect your photographs to be looked at in the light of this?

Edward: When I take photographs I know it's a moment now, but I am also aware that the photographs themselves will become history. I spent some weeks with the photographer Sergei Chilikov when I was a student. We would go out photographing and he would point at a shop window and say 'museum!' He would then point at the road and say 'museum!'. I think what he was suggesting, at least the way I interpreted it, was that with documentary photography the whole world is *your museum*. You are able to show people what you saw in it. A photograph exists outside of time and therein lies its inherent magic. I think most people have forgotten that. When I photograph I feel omnipresent. The photograph of Nigel Farage in the book laughing in front of the giant word 'Good' is ironic. It is made whilst I was conscious of how some people will see that moment looking back at it.

David: Are you optimistic about the future that will look back at the image of Farage?

Edward: I think with time we, humanity, generally end up looking back and seeing the right side of history, don't we? It's just always difficult in the moment. I hope the person reading our conversation in 2041 can see the irony of the Brexit Party all laughing at the word Good now that humanity has learned we are better together and how to love one another. I do, however, have a slight

Valencia, Spain (1933) Henri Cartier-Bresson

paranoia about some future frontpage of the Daily Mail where that photograph is used to celebrate the glorious beginning of Brexit.... No, there is no way that's going to happen. Even if it did, I wouldn't sell them the photograph.

David: What you say does point us to the fact that there is not going to be one way to read these photographs. Ambiguity is part of their power and their risk, no?

Edward: People see what they want to see. This is always the way; the photographs reflect the viewers own prejudices. In the past I've had the same photograph co-opted as memes by both far-right and far-left groups. It's a common issue in documentary photography. In the beginning I aligned myself to make the 'one image tells all' photographs that came out of the British documentary tradition of the 1980's. A day spent having beers with Richard Billingham in Margate when I was 23 years old changed my approach. I mentioned the iconic image of his late father pictured with what looks like a giant bottle of beer and his mother looking sternly at him, I was surprised when he said that it was his least favourite photograph. This made me re-evaluate what I thought about photography. Diane Arbus once said, a photograph is a secret about a secret, the more it tells you the less you know. If there is ambiguity in the photographs, I hope the sequencing and placement of photographs within the book helps to convey my own feelings. There are certain pairings of images that aim to be reflexive, but two diptychs are worth mentioning

as they are connected. The first is of St George walking along a high street paired with a St George tattoo on the back of an E.D.L protestor. The second is of British Tommy living historians paired with a tattoo of a Poppy on another E.D.L protestor. In both instances I am trying to break the third wall of the photo book – giving the viewer the impression that the people in the photographs are aware they are in a photo book. That they are looking across onto the opposite page and that they are somewhat unimpressed by what they see. They are now able to look out of England's past, both its mythology and history, to lay judgement on the present and those that take their iconography for their own misjudged purposes.

David: Were you photographing what made you feel ambiguous?

Edward: I know they made me feel something at the time. It's like recognising something you don't know yet, like déjà vu. This is what I think is a bit like sagacity, not knowing what I am looking for with my camera until I find it. I think there's some value in that. It is like a way of being humble. Being open to experiences and what may happen, and within that space, finding what you were meant to find.

I was never a fan of press photography or assignments where you had to point the camera at 'the thing you are supposed to photograph'. I prefer to rely on my own perception and instincts. Maybe there are certain

moments that are ambiguous and defy a clear explanation and that's what seemed interesting to me, but in myself, even in the anxious hyper-active state I'm in when I photograph, I am very focused and confident. The photograph of the boy blinded by the sun in this book, for me, echoes a famous early career photograph by Henri Cartier-Bresson of a small boy looking up, his back against a wall. It's uncharacteristic of Cartier-Bresson's work, it's not a decisive moment at all, it's something else. It's not easy to explain. The difference in content between a postcard and a novel.

David: For all its common use as a medium of supposedly functional communication, the medium's forte may well be how it allows a photographer and a viewer the opportunity for mixed feelings. A fixed image but an unfixed response. It's interesting what you mentioned about the editing and the sequencing of the book being a way of structuring those mixed feelings, if not exactly resolving them.

Edward: Indeed, 'a fixed image and an unfixed response'. I'd say this goes even further in that our response to a photograph is always unfixed too. The photograph, with its ability to freeze a moment in time, renders the viewer the ability to look back again and again over the course of their lives. We change and so our response to the photograph changes. It's like reading the same book over and over again during your lifetime. You will notice different things. One of the last photographs in this book, of the writing saying 'I love you forever' had a deeply personal meaning for me. When the photograph was taken in 2009 it was the 2nd anniversary of my father's death and that is the spot where his ashes were scattered. To me, it was like a message from beyond the grave. Re-visiting that photograph in 2016 it took on another meaning - the sea mist over the English Channel is now obscuring the coast of France, the graffiti has become a love letter to Europe in post-Brexit Britain. Now viewing the photograph since 2019 I am now a father to twin girls and there they are standing on their scooters looking out to sea, perhaps where my own ashes will be scattered one day.

David: How far into the years of shooting were you before you began to think about making a book? Did the prospect of making a book inform the kind of photographs you were taking?

Edward: This book started five years ago when I moved back to Kent. I started with an edit of my best work shot in the county but after the referendum I saw a connection to the themes in my previous photo-essays to many of the catalysts of Brexit: Nostalgia culture, the rise of populism, our still ever-present class system and xenophobia. This then guided the edit of my archive. There's a lot of new work made in the past five years, that's how it really came together. I think a book just about Kent would have still been relevant, but I wanted to do something that really reflected the current climate. Many of the key images in the book were made in London and other counties, so it had to be England as

a whole. I'm trying to say something more than just this is the garden of England. That's why the book is called what it is. But it isn't a Brexit book either. Over twenty years my visual style has stayed the same, so photographs made in 2021 look like they could have been made in 2001. Some of the photographs look genuinely anachronistic because they are of re-enactors or retro-socialisers. But many of the photographs in the book seem like they were photographed during different decades. The Miss Faversham float photograph could have been from the Eighties, the Extinction Rebellion protestors from the Sixties. This ties in with my philosophy of being able to photograph outside of time. I am conscious that the photograph I make will exist separately from our ongoing timeline, at the moment I capture the photograph I am also outside of time. If you can exist outside of time then the past, present and future become one.

David: What was the last image you shot for the book?

Edward: The very last photograph I made that is in the book was photographed this year (2021) and is of the topiary man. It is actually very near to where I live, which is probably why I never got round to photographing it before. As I was taking the photograph a passerby stopped to chat, he told me that the man who planted it and pruned it for 30 years had just died. For me the topiary sculpture is mythological, it hits that British folk horror note too. It's the Fat Controller, its Bertie Bassett, it's the Green Man. I think it is a worthy edition to the

book as its indicative of that kind of British eccentric, a person who starts doing a crazy thing one day which they end up doing their whole life.

David: It's interesting that in myths of national identity around the world there is a place for the obsessive outsider who carries on indifferent to what's going on around then. Maybe it's because it's kind of noble in a blind way, but it's also insular in its disregard. But the obsessiveness of the observational photographer is different because it does require a world to photograph, even if it's only to mirror back the observer's obsessions. After working on your project for such a long time has it been difficult to bring it to a conclusion and let it go?

Edward: This series had to finish to allow me to make new work. I have three very esoteric photography projects I want to work on. One I've been waiting nearly 10 years to begin. I'd like to start making documentary films too, I think thats a logical progression. But this kind of photography will always be my first love. There are photographs in this book of my next-door neighbours, close friends, my late father, that's how close I am to some of the work. Letting go is difficult, but I think Covid and the global pandemic has made us enter a new epoch. All of the work in this book made from 2002 - 2020 is from that former time.

IN-A-GADDA-DA-ENGLAND
EDWARD THOMPSON
First Edition
Limited 500 copies
Offset Printed
Flying Camera Publishing 2022
ISBN 978-1-7397816-0-6

Editioned photographic prints from this book are available from: www.edwardthompson.co.uk

I would like to thank:

Anyone who gave me work freelancing as a photographer, bought a print or got me
teaching work. You kept me afloat. Dr Paul Lowe for being the first photographer who
really believed in me. Dr Lewis Bush for ripping off my worst ideas so I didn't need to make
them, his counsel, bowling skills and friendship. Dr Sally Waterman for help editing the
crowdfunding video and copy editing the texts in the book. Everyone who crowdfunded this
book, without even one of you (it was that close) this book wouldn't have been made. Miles
Fraser, Rav Singh and Bethany Chater for their help with the crowdfunding video. Mark
Makela for his never-ending belief in my photography, spurring me on so many times when
I had quit, giving me assignments (other photographers never do this) and general energy.
To the photographic *Ken to my Ryu*, Ben Speck, we shared the same masters. Jan-Joseph
Stok, the closest I've ever come to meeting the true spirit of the humanitarian photojournalist
in my lifetime. Claudia Leisinger for her support, abhorrence to bullshit and wisdom. Homer
Sykes for being the only old guard photographer who ever invited me into his home and
made lunch. Fiona Shields for looking at a very early edit of this work. Jocelyn Bain Hogg
for becoming excited enough to call someone while looking at my work, no idea who it was,
but it was a lovely gesture to a young photographer. For Peter Dench for being Peter Dench.
Dr Francis Summers for his feedback on the book and guiding me to a higher path with it.
Heike Lowenstein for being the first course leader to give me a real break into teaching, you
changed my life. Maggie Pinhorn for showing my Occupy London work at the East London
Photo Festival all those years ago and getting me to do my first ever talk at The Bishopsgate
Institute. Louise Francis & Laura Knight for their support in the early years. Paul Jackson for
making the illustration for this book and lending me his dad after my dad had passed away.
Sergei Chilikov for being a wild and wise old bear, R.I.P. Tricky Trev who gave me my first
job as a holiday camp photographer, who t-cut the bonnet of my old Polo outside his trailer
home. All the students I've studied alongside and taught, in this ever more anti-intellectual
world of philistines, you are the brave. May you be rewarded with the golden insights of
unfettered truth. David Campany for generously undertaking the gruelling three day email
exchange for the books Q&A. The band T.V Priest for using a photograph from the book as
their album artwork. The Idle Hand Society podcast and Small Voice Podcast for their help
in getting the word out. My ex-K.I.A.D crew including Liam, Asa, Joe, Gav, Sean and James
for their love, memes and care. Luke Brown for his camera dealing. My brother for lending
(giving) me his Pentax K1000 in the mid 90's and starting this whole thing off. My friend
Stefan for being my first muse. My mum for her selfless-ness, her grace and love. My dad
for his graft, his wisdom and for bringing me He-Man figures whenever he came back from
working in Shetland. My dearest Ros and my beautiful girls - if this book is a documentation
of a life lived, then you are the purpose of that life. I love you with all my heart and soul.

In-A-Gadda-Da-England illustration in graphite (2021) Paul Jackson ©
Valencia, Spain (1933) Henri Cartier-Bresson © Foundation Henri Cartier-Bresson
Kensington Children's party (1934) Bill Brandt © Bill Brandt Archive